Legacy of War

Legacy of War

◆

Profiles of the 67 brave young men from Evansville, IN who perished in the Vietnam War

D. Samuel Melchior

iUniverse, Inc.
New York Bloomington Shanghai

Legacy of War
Profiles of the 67 brave young men from Evansville, IN who perished in the Vietnam War

Copyright © 2008 by David Samuel Melchior

All rights reserved. No part of this book may be used or reproduced by any means, graphic, electronic, or mechanical, including photocopying, recording, taping or by any information storage retrieval system without the written permission of the publisher except in the case of brief quotations embodied in critical articles and reviews.

iUniverse books may be ordered through booksellers or by contacting:

iUniverse
1663 Liberty Drive
Bloomington, IN 47403
www.iuniverse.com
1-800-Authors (1-800-288-4677)

Because of the dynamic nature of the Internet, any Web addresses or links contained in this book may have changed since publication and may no longer be valid.

The views expressed in this work are solely those of the author and do not necessarily reflect the views of the publisher, and the publisher hereby disclaims any responsibility for them.

ISBN: 978-0-595-50222-6 (pbk)
ISBN: 978-0-595-61421-9 (ebk)

Printed in the United States of America

Contents

Acknowledgements vii
Introduction xi
Casualty Profiles-Original 1
"The Other Side" 57
Casualty Profiles—The Other Side 58
Evansville's Vietnam Casualties by High School 70
Evansville Vietnam Era Casualties by Military Unit 72
MOS Codes-Vietnam Era 76
About the Proceeds Beneficiaries 78
About the Vietnam Veterans Memorial-Washington D.C. 80
Conclusion 83
Sources 85

Acknowledgements

It is not possible to give thanks to the soldiers that gave their all for our country, but this book is dedicated to these young men from Evansville that perished in the Vietnam War. I learned the lesson of how a simple thank you is sorely inadequate from a student I had in an eight-grade history class. She offered the following in response to a Thanksgiving Day assignment I gave one year. It was so good I submitted it to the Evansville Courier and Press and it was the lead letter to the editor on Thanksgiving Day.

Dear Veteran,

I was given this assignment to thank you, though I've recently found out that in no way is that possible. My ignorance of the intensity of war has fortunately been replaced with knowledge that has enabled me to clearly see that the simple phrase "thank you", which is commonly used for just the act of opening a door and such, has almost no meaning when expressed to heroes such as you.

Because of this I have repeatedly asked myself, how can the American people show their appreciation, love, honor, and respect to the heroic people who have truly stepped up for our country? The answer I've come up with expressed the idea that although it is nearly impossible to show these thoughts and emotions through words spoken or written, they should be seen by you and all veterans by what we as Americans are able to have and do.

You should honor yourselves, because if it weren't for you, the American way of life would not exist as it does today. So although there really is no way to ever repay or express our feelings of thanks, just know that it is there, and because of you the American people will live the life that was intended for them to live.

After having read this, all I could think was, "Wow." I could not say it any better.

I would also like to thank Jan Scruggs and the Vietnam Veterans Memorial staff for all their encouragement to teachers through their conferences, website and free teaching materials. Also thanks for the wonderful opportunities to travel to Vietnam and experience the rich culture of this vibrant country.

Thanks to the Evansville Public Library for their on-line data bases that made the research for this book possible. Charles Browning of Browning Funeral Home created the main database used. His tireless work in cataloging local history events has kept alive stories that otherwise would have been lost forever.

I want to thank the many students of Christa McAuliffe Middle School who helped with the initial research in the 2002–03 school year.

Thank you to Dr. Gregory Brown, the principal who hired me to work in alternative education in 1992. I could not have pursued the many projects over the years, including this one without his encouragement and support.

Thank you to Mark Acker, the post commander of VFW 1114, the largest post in the country, which is located in Evansville. Mark was instrumental in getting a new Vietnam Memorial project off the ground. He has supported this project and provided information on some of the men in this book.

Thank you to my friend and colleague Bill Phelps for all the stories about his time in Vietnam. Also to Jim "colonel" Maroney for recounting his time spent during the war and his beautiful art work for the cover.

Thanks to my wife Becky and children Tyler and Cameron for their support and encouragement in my travels.

Finally, I want to bestow a special dedication to Becky's sister, Jennifer Solomon, who exemplifies the words courage and strength. You can read about Jenny on the beneficiaries' page.

"For the Soldiers"

Introduction

"I guess that's the great sadness to war, the plants, the flowers, the trees all grow back, but people don't" (Dennis Mannion, Khe Sahn veteran; *A Walk in the Clouds*). Mannion's quote is so matter of fact and to the point it becomes difficult to expand on what legacy war leaves behind. The simple fact that young people die violent deaths, often in far away places, should strike a nerve in most people, and make them see that war should be avoided whenever possible. Waging war on others should be carefully thought out and all diplomatic avenues explored before it is decided there is no alternative. With that being said, it is not an overt intention of this work to editorialize about war in general, but to simply attempt to demonstrate that the profound and far-reaching effects of war may actually be greater than previously believed. Certainly this premise may be challenged especially by those directly affected by war, such as veterans and their families. My thoughts on the more far-reaching effects are based on my experience as a civilian. I think most people from Evansville, veterans and civilians, will find someone they know in this book.

Thirty years after the end of the Vietnam War I found myself on the brink of a-once-in-a-lifetime opportunity. I was part of a group that traveled to Vietnam to raise awareness of a humanitarian project sponsored by the Vietnam Veterans Memorial Fund (VVMF). My involvement stems from the VVMF, which sponsored a conference in the summer of 2002 for teachers to become involved with educating about the War and the Vietnam Memorial Wall in Washington, D.C. By attending the conference, teachers became part of the Teach Vietnam Teachers' Network. Then in 2005 we were invited to take part in raising awareness for Project Renew by traveling to Vietnam as a delegation of concerned Americans. This project, sponsored by the VVMF, is designed to help rid Quang Tri Province of leftover unexploded ordnance (UXO) from the Vietnam War. These mines and bombs are still killing and maiming thirty years later.

The responsibility that went along with becoming a member of the teachers' network was to complete a community project about the Vietnam War. My choice of project was to rededicate our local Vietnam War Memorial, which is one of the oldest in the country. It was originally dedicated on January 29, 1973, just two days after the signing of the Paris Peace Treaty officially ending hostilities between North Vietnam and the United States. I became aware of the memorial's existence as a result of joining the network. I was not aware of this memorial before and I found that many Vietnam veterans are still not aware of it. There are simple reasons for this. One is that it is somewhat hidden and consists of just a small tombstone with brass plaques on either side with the names of the fallen soldiers. It sits at the corner of Martin Luther King Blvd. and Main Street in Evansville, IN. The unpopularity of the war and many veterans wanting to just forget about the war is another reason this memorial is often forgotten. The fact that it is so old also makes it easily overlooked.

On April 22, 2003 students at my school, Christa McAuliffe Middle School, helped lead a rededication of the memorial, commemorating its thirtieth anniversary. Because of that rededication I became interested in finding out more about the men listed on the memorial, thus the impetus for this project. As I began researching I found a variety of information on the war casualties. It ranged from not much more than the soldier's name and basic military information, to the amazing history of Tom Metsker. Metsker is portrayed in the book "We were soldiers once—and young" and the subsequent movie. As I delved into the background of the memorial I found there was some controversy over a plaque that was added to the other side of the memorial in November of 1973. This little bit of controversy is explained after the profiles of the original fifty-five soldiers. Because of the range of biographical information available this should be considered a work in progress. I welcome any new information and when enough is collected I would like to print updated versions.

The following profiles, along with the UXO issues in Vietnam, and life-long challenges faced by surviving veterans of the Vietnam War, both American and Vietnamese, comprise an awesomely sad legacy of lost lives, potential, and opportunities.

Casualty Profiles-Original

William L. Armstrong

Military Information:

MOS: 11B20

Casualty Date: Sun. Feb. 6, 1966

Length of Tour: 23 Days

On the Wall: Panel 05E, Line 005

Grade: E4

Service: Marine Corps, Regular

Tour of Duty Began: Sat. 1/8/1966

Casualty Place: Province and Military Region Unknown, South Vietnam

Casualty Type: Hostile, Died, Multiple Fragmentation Wounds, Ground Casualty

Personal Information:

Born: Fri. July 6, 1945

Religion: Other, Not Reported

Age at Casualty Date: 20

Marital Status: Single

Race: Negro

Service Entry Point: Evansville, IN

High School: Central High School, 1964 Grad.

Other Information: I did not find Armstrong's high school information until I received his Individual Deceased Personnel File (IDPF) from the Marine Corps. These files are public record, but are difficult to get in a timely manner and are expensive if more than two are ordered at a time. At the time of this writing I have obtained two IDPF files. In Armstrong's IDPF file it mentioned that he had a Central yearbook among his personal property. By chance at the beginning of this school year we had a substitute teacher that is a Vietnam veteran. I was telling him about this book and he asked me if Billy Armstrong would be part of it. It continues to amaze me how many people know these men.

Evansville History Fact: In 1959 Evansville College wins its first NCAA Division II Championship in basketball.

Robert Lee Baker

Military Information:	Grade: E4
MOS: 11B20	Service: Army, Regular
Casualty Date: Fri., May 10, 1968	Tour of Duty Began: Thu. 1/11/1968
Length of Tour: 120 Days	Casualty Place: Kontim, South Vietnam

On the Wall: Panel 58E, Line 003

Casualty Type: Hostile, Died, Multiple Fragmentation Wounds, Ground Casualty

Personal Information:

Born: Tue. Sep. 28, 1948	Marital Status: Single
Religion: Protestant, No Preference	Race: Caucasian
Age at Casualty Date: 19	Service Entry Point: Evansville, IN
High School: Reitz High School	

Other Information: Robert Baker had been wounded two months before his death. He received fragmentation wounds to the face but was able to return to duty. In a newspaper article his mother spoke of the many letters he sent home about how scary Vietnam was.

Evansville History Fact: Frank McDonald is elected Mayor of Evansville in 1960.

James Lisman Blackwell, Jr.

Military Information:

MOS: 1542

Casualty Date: Tue. Oct. 17, 1967

Length of Tour: 67 Days

Grade: Capt./O3

Service: Army, Regular

Tour of Duty Began: Sat. 08/05/1967

Casualty Place: Binh Long, South Vietnam

On The Wall: Panel 28E, Line 019

Casualty Type: Hostile, Died, Gun, Small Arms Fire, Ground Casualty

Personal Information:

Born: Fri. Dec 27, 1940

Religion: Presbyterian

Age at Casualty Date: 26

High School: Reitz High School

Marital Status: Married

Race: Caucasian

Service Entry Point: Evansville, IN

Other Information: James Blackwell was a West Point graduate and career soldier. He volunteered for Vietnam duty. Blackwell had a six-month-old son at the time of his death. He was killed one day after Larry Stotler, another Evansville soldier, was killed.

Evansville History Fact: In 1960 Evansville College wins its second NCAA Division II Championship in basketball.

Stephen Bruce Boehne

Military Information:

MOS: 11B40

Casualty Date: Fri. Mar. 13, 1970

Length of Tour: 181 Days

Grade: SSGT/E6

Service: Army, Selective Service

Tour of Duty Began: Sat. 9/13/1969

Casualty Place: Quang Ngai, South Vietnam

On The Wall: Panel 13W, Line 122

Casualty Type: Hostile, Died, Other Explosive Device, Ground Casualty

Personal Information:

Born: Mon. Nov. 15, 1948

Religion: Lutheran & Missouri Synod

Age at Casualty Date: 21

Marital Status Single

Race: Caucasian

Service Entry Point: Evansville, IN

High School: Bosse High School, 1966 Grad.

Other Information: Stephen Boehne was killed by a booby trap while on a combat mission with a new unit. According to Boehne's father he was originally with the First Army Division and was scheduled to come home but was reassigned to the new unit.

Vietnam History Fact: On November 30, 1961 President Kennedy authorizes the use of the defoliant Agent Orange in Vietnam.

John Edward Bohnsack

Military Information:

MOS: 11B20

Casualty Date: Sat. Nov. 6, 1965

Length of Tour: 87 Days

Grade: LTC/05

Service: Army Reserve

Tour of Duty Began: 8/20/1965

Casualty Place: Province and Military Region Unknown, South Vietnam

On The Wall: Panel 32W, Line 036

Casualty Type: Non-Hostile, Died of illness/injury, Heart Attack, Ground casualty

Personal Information:

Born: Thu. Nov. 28, 1929

Religion: Evangelical United Brethren

Age at Casualty Date: 39

High School: Bosse High School

Marital Status: Single

Race: Caucasian

Service Entry Point: Evansville, IN

Other Information: John Bohnsack was a finance officer and was attending a meeting in Saigon when he became ill. It was determined he suffered a heart attack. He had no history of heart problems.

Evansville History Fact: Harrison High School opens in 1962.

Byron Dean Bonds

Military Information:

MOS: 0311

Casualty Date: Fri. Apr. 21, 1967

Length of Tour: Cannot Determine

Grade: LCPL/E3

Service: Marine Corps, Regular

Tour of Duty Began: Not Reported

Casualty Place: Quang Nam, South Vietnam

On The Wall: Panel 18E, Line 056

Casualty Type: Hostile, Died, Gun, Small Arms Fire, Ground Casualty

Personal Information:

Born: Sat. Nov 23, 1946

Religion: Protestant, No Preference

Age at Casualty Date: 20

High School: Reitz High School

Marital Status: Single

Race: Caucasian

Service Entry Point: Evansville, IN

Other Information: Byron Bonds had a brother and four sisters at the time of his death.

Evansville History Fact: In 1963 Washington Square Mall opens to become the first enclosed shopping center in Indiana.

Lewis Eli Bonnie

Military Information:

MOS: Not Reported

Casualty Date: Tue. Nov. 8, 1966

Length of Tour: 82 Days

Grade: SFC/E7

Service: Army Regular

Tour of Duty Began: 8/18/1966

Casualty Place: Province and Military Region Unknown, South Vietnam

On The Wall: Panel 12E, Line 040

Casualty Type: Hostile, Died, Gun, Small Arms Fire, Ground Casualty

Personal Information:

Born: Tue July 22, 1930

Religion: Methodist

Age at Casualty Date: 36

High School: Unknown

Marital Status: Married

Race: Caucasian

Service Entry Point: Evansville, IN

Other Information: Lewis Bonnie was married and had three children at the time of his death.

Evansville History Fact: In 1963 Evansville Airport was declared one of the top ten small hub airports in the country.

Terry Wayne Booker

Military Information:

MOS: 0311

Casualty Date: Thu. Oct. 9, 1969

Length of Tour: 321 Days

Grade: PFC/E2

Service: Marine Corps, Regular

Tour of Duty Began: 11/23/1968

Casualty Place: Quang Tri, South Vietnam

On The Wall: Panel 17W, Line 054

Casualty Type: Hostile, Died, Other Explosive Device, Ground Casualty

Personal Information:

Born: Tue. Sep 19, 1950

Religion: Protestant, No Preference

Age at Casualty Date: 19

High School: Harrison High School

Marital Status: Single

Race: Caucasian

Service Entry Point: Evansville, IN

Other Information: Booker had received the Purple Heart earlier in his tour when he was wounded when the truck in which he was riding hit a landmine.

Vietnam History Fact: On July 10, 1964 the first soldier with Evansville ties, Leonard Wayne Lockard, is killed in Vietnam when his helicopter crashes.

James Wisdom Bowling

Military Information:

MOS: 0311	Grade: PFC/E2
Casualty Date: Sat. Dec 7, 1968	Service: Marine Corps, Regular
Length of Tour: 290 Days	Tour of Duty Began: 02/21/1968
	Casualty Place: Quang Nam, South Vietnam

On The Wall: Panel 13W, Line 122

Casualty Type: Hostile, Died, Gun, Small Arm Fire, Ground Casualty

Personal Information:

Born: Sat. Apr. 24, 1948	Marital Status: Single
Religion: Protestant, No Preference	Race: Negro
Age at Casualty Date: 20	Service Entry Point: Evansville, IN
High School: Bosse High School	

Other Information: Bowling had planned to get married in February of 1969.

Vietnam History Fact: On August 6, 1964 Lt. Everett Alvarez Jr. becomes the first American POW in Vietnam after being shot down in a raid on North Vietnamese bases.

Kenneth R. Bowman

Note: Two of the names on the Evansville, IN Vietnam Memorial are not considered official Vietnam casualties. Bowman is one of them. Very little is known at this point about Bowman. I have found no military records and very little local information about him.

Evansville History Fact: In 1964 Evansville College wins its third NCAA Division II championship in basketball.

Vietnam Veterans of the 2005 delegation at the DMZ

Chester Briscoe, Jr.

Military Information:

MOS: 1371

Casualty Date: Sat. May 25, 1968

Length of Tour: 110 Days

Grade: PFC/E2

Service: Marine Corps, Regular

Tour of Duty Began: 2/4/1968

Casualty Place: Quang Tri, South Vietnam

On The Wall: Panel 69W, Line 001

Casualty Type: Hostile, Died, Gun, Small Arms Fire, Ground Casualty

Personal Information:

Born: Sep. 28, 1948

Religion: Protestant, No preference

Age at Casualty Date: 19

Marital Status: Single

Race: Negro

Service Entry point: Evansville, IN

High School: Reitz High School

Other information: Briscoe's father was a veteran of World War II. When I contacted Mark Acker of VFW 1114 he told me of his acquaintance with Briscoe. They had attended Reitz High School together.

Vietnam History Fact: On March 2, 1965 the Vietnam War heats up with the start of Operation Rolling Thunder bombing campaign on North Vietnam. The United States had conducted bombing raids on North Vietnam as early as December of 1964.

Jeffrey Lynn Buchanan

Military Information:

MOS: 0311

Casualty Date: Thu. Nov. 14, 1968

Length of Tour: 313 Days

Grade: PFC/E2

Service: Marine Corps, Regular

Tour of Duty Began: 1/5/1968

Casualty Place: Quang Tri, South Vietnam

On The Wall: Panel 39W, Line 064

Casualty Type: Hostile, Died, Artillery, Rocket, Mortar, Ground Casualty

Personal Information:

Born: Thu. Feb 17, 1949

Religion: Roman Catholic

Age at Casualty Date: 19

School: Harrison High School, 1967 Grad.

Marital Status: Single

Race: Caucasian

Service Entry Point: Evansville, IN

Other Information: When our school rededicated our local memorial Buchanan's cousin, Kathy Godeke, attended and was the focus of an article in the Evansville Courier and Press the next day.

Vietnam History Fact: On March 8, 1965 the first American combat force of 3500 marines arrive in Vietnam at DaNang.

John Gary Buchanan

Military Information:

MOS: 100B

Casualty Date: Thu. Dec. 24, 1970

Length of Tour: 87 Days

Grade: WO/W1

Service: Army, Reserve

Tour of Duty Began: 9/29/1970

Casualty Place: Binh Duong, South Vietnam

On The Wall: Panel 05W, Line 004

Casualty Type: Non-Hostile, Died of other causes, Air Loss, Crash, Helicopter, Crew

Personal Information:

Born: Thu. May 9, 1946

Religion: Presbyterian

Age at Casualty Date: 24

High School: North High School

Marital Status: Married

Race: Caucasian

Service Entry Point: Evansville, IN

Other Information: Buchanan's wife was expecting their daughter when he was killed. His daughter went on to become the wife of an officer in the United States Navy. Buchanan was also a graduate of Evansville College.

Evansville History Fact: In 1964 Evansville College wins its fourth NCAA Division II championship in basketball.

Robert Clewlow

Military Information:	Grade: SGT/E5
MOS: 11B4P	Service: Army, Selective Service
Casualty Date: Sat. Mar 9, 1968	Tour of Duty Began: 12/13/1967
Length of Tour: 86 Days	Casualty Place: Thua Thien, South Vietnam

On The Wall: Panel 43E, Line 066

Casualty Type: Hostile, Died, Multiple Fragmentation Wounds, Ground Casualty

Personal Information:

Born: Thu. Dec. 2, 1948	Marital Status: Single
Religion: Baptist, Other Groups	Race: Caucasian
Age at Casualty Date: 19	Service Entry Point: Evansville, IN
High School: Harrison High School	

Other Information: Robert had a brother in the National Guard at the time of his death.

Evansville History Fact: In 1965 Indiana University was given the excavation rights to Angel Mounds Native American archaeological site by the Indiana Historical Society.

William Stanley Daugherty

Military Information:

Grade: LCPL/E3

MOS: 0341

Service: Marine Corps, Regular

Casualty Date: Sat. June 3, 1967

Tour of Duty Began: 12/26/1966

Length of Tour: 134 Days

Casualty Place: Quang Tin, South Vietanm

On The Wall: Panel 21E, Line 043

Casualty Type: Hostile, Died, Gun, Small Arms Fire, Ground Casualty

Personal Information:

Born: Mar. 2, 1948

Marital Status: Single

Religion: Protestant, No Preference

Race: Caucasian

Age at Casualty Date: 19

Service Entry Point: Evansville, IN

High School: Central High School, 1966 Grad.

Other information: Daugherty was a friend of Bruce Mielke who was also killed while serving in Vietnam later that year on August 1. Mielke was never informed of Daugherty's death. They had attended Central High School together.

Evansville History Fact: In September of 1965 Indiana State University Evansville opens as a regional campus of Indiana State University.

Gene Edmond Davis

Military Information:

MOS: 43191

Casualty Date: Thu, Jan 24, 1974*

Length of Tour: Cannot Determine

Grade: CMS/E8

Service: Air Force, Regular

Tour of Duty Began: 3/13/1966

Casualty Place: Kontum, South Vietnam

On The Wall: Panel 06E, Line 005

Casualty Type: Hostile, Died while missing, Air Loss, Crash, Fixed Wing, Crew

Personal Information:

Born: Thu. Apr. 5, 1928

Religion: Baptist, Other Groups

Age at casualty Date: 45

High School: Reitz High School

Marital Status: Married

Race: Caucasian

Service Entry Point: Evansville, IN

Other Information: Gene Davis was a flight master on a C47. Originally Davis was MIA so the actual date of death is not known although the date of the crash is the same as Davis's start of duty date. The mission was armed reconnaissance along route 92 west of Da Nang.

*He was officially declared killed on this date. His remains have not been recovered.

Vietnam History Fact: By December of 1965 180,000 troops are serving in Vietnam.

Anthony William Dean

Military Information:

MOS: 11B4P

Casualty Date: Tue. Dec. 9, 1969

Length of Tour: 29 Days

Grade: SGT/E5

Service: Army, Regular

Tour of Duty Began: 11/11/1969

Casualty Place: Quang Ngai, South Vietnam

On The Wall: Panel 15W, Line 041

Casualty Type: Hostile, Died, Gun, Small Arms Fire, Ground Casualty

Personal Information:

Born: Fri., Mar. 18, 1949

Religion: Lutheran & Missouri Synod

Age at Casualty Date: 20

High School: Central High School

Marital Status, Married

Race: Caucasian

Service Entry Point: Evansville, IN

Other Information: Anthony Dean had a 22-month-old son at the time of his death. He was a 3 year starter on the Central football team and was named the offensive lineman of the year his senior season. He was named first team all-city and second-team all conference.

Vietnam History Fact: By August of 1966 292,000 troops are in Vietnam.

Ronald Lee Dempsey

Military Information:
MOS: 3531
Casualty Date: Wed. Feb. 28, 1968
Length of Tour: 248 Days

Grade: CPL/E4
Service: Marine Corps, Regular
Tour of Duty Began: 6/25/1967
Casualty Place: Quang Tri, South Vietnam

On The Wall: Panel 41E, Line 063
Casualty Type: Hostile, Died, Air Loss, Crash, Helicopter, Non-crew

Personal Information:
Born: Mon. Dec. 8, 1947
Religion: Protestant, No Preference
Age at Casualty Date: 20

Marital Status: Single
Race: Caucasian
Service Entry Point: Evansville, IN

High School: North High School, 1965 Grad.

Other Information: When I was accepted into the Teach Vietnam Teachers' Network, Ron's name was picked by the VVMF staff as the person I was to honor at a ceremony during our conference. Consequently I found quite a bit of information on Ron. I e-mailed a war buddy who had left a remembrance on the VVMF website. His name is Cliff Trease and was featured on the History Channel program Unsung heroes, the battle of Khe Sanh. Ron's helicopter was shot down while they were on a recovery mission near the embattled combat base at Khe Sanh. According to reports this was Dempsey's second tour. Between tours Ron had come home and joined the VFW. Ron's name was also part of a war protest when an eighteen year old from Michigan wore a placard around his neck at a protest in Washington, D.C. with Ron's name printed on it. The Michigan youth did not know Ron. The year of the conference I attempted to contact Ron's mother as she was still listed in the phone book at the address where Ron grew up. She never returned my calls. My guess is that the pain of the loss was just too great for her to speak to a stranger about it. At that point I decided to limit my research to public records and newspaper accounts and sometimes friends of mine that might have known some of these men. If a family member approached me, as did Jeffrey Buchanan's cousin I would of course acquire information.

Vietnam History Fact: On October 26, 1966 President Johnson visited U.S. troops in Vietnam.

Ordnance disposal worker at UXO site, Quang Tri, Vietnam

Michael Earl Dent

Military Information:

MOS: 11B20

Casualty Date: Sat. Dec 17, 1966

Length of Tour: 97 Days

Grade: E3

Service: Army, Regular

Tour of Duty Began: 9/1/1966

Casualty Place: Province and Military Region Unknown, South Vietnam

On The Wall: Panel 13E, Line 051

Casualty Type: Hostile, Died, Gun, Small Arms Fire, Ground Casualty

Personal Information:

Born: Tue. Dec. 16, 1947

Religion: Latter Day Saints, Mormon

Age at Casualty Date: 19

High School: Unknown

Marital Status: Single

Race: Caucasian

Service Entry Point: Evansville, IN

Other Information: Note that Michael Dent was killed the day after his birthday.

Vietnam History Fact: During the year 1967 the number of in-country troops reaches 500,000.

Ronald Lee Ellis

Military Information:

MOS: 0311

Casualty Date: Wed. Mar. 8, 1968

Length of Tour: 281 Days

Grade: CPL/E4

Service: Marine Corps, Regular

Tour of Duty Began: 5/25/1967

Casualty Place: Quang Tri, South Vietnam

On The Wall: Panel 43E, Line 017

Casualty Type: Hostile, Died, Gun, Small Arms Fire, Ground Casualty

Personal Information:

Born: Fri. Oct. 17, 1947

Religion: Protestant, No Preference

Age at Casualty Date: 20

High School: North High School

Marital Status: Single

Race: Caucasian

Service Entry Point: Evansville, IN

Other Information: Ellis's story is one of the most poignant because he wrote a short letter to his mother the day he was killed. Due to incredible timing his mother found out about his death while at work and later that day when she got home the letter had arrived in the mail. He commented in his letter how bad things were getting and how he would be on his way home in eighty days.

Evansville History Fact: In 1967 Evansville College officially becomes University of Evansville.

Robert Mathew Fegan

Military Information:

MOS: 2P40	Grade: SFC/E7
Casualty Date: Wed. June 18, 1969	Service: Army, Regular
Length of Tour: 167 Days	Tour of Duty Began: 1/3/1969
	Casualty Place: Thua Thien, South Vietnam

On The Wall: Panel 22W, Line 076

Casualty Type: Non-Hostile, Died of Other Causes, Accident, Ground Casualty

Personal Information:

Born: Sun. Nov. 9, 1930	Marital Status; Married
Religion: Presbyterian	Race: Caucasian
Age at Casualty date: 38	Service Entry Point: Evansville, IN
High School: North High School	

Other Information: Matthew Fegan's death was a mystery. He was found on the runway at Phu Bai Airport. A newspaper article indicated an autopsy would be ordered. I was unable to find a follow up on that article. Later the military stated the death was accidental. Fegan was an accomplished musician and played the trombone.

Evansville History Fact: In 1967 the Southern Indiana Higher Education Commission raised nearly $1,000,000 to purchase 1400 acres for the Indiana State University Evansville campus.

David Frank Garrett

Military Information:

MOS: 0311

Casualty Date: Thu. Sep. 21, 1967

Length of Tour: 94 Days

Grade: LCPL/E3

Service: Marine Corps, Regular

Tour of Duty Began: 6/20/1967

Casualty Place: Quang Tri, South Vietnam

On The Wall: Panel 26E, Line 101

Casualty Type: Hostile, Died, Gun, Small Arms Fire

Personal Information:

Born: Sun. Dec. 28, 1947

Religion: Roman Catholic

Age at Casualty Date: 19

High School: Rex Mundi High School

Marital Status: Single

Race Caucasian

Service Entry Point: Evansville, IN

Other Information: David Garrett was posthumously award the Bronze Star with V for Valor. The award stated under enemy fire he crawled to an injured soldier to render aid when he was mortally wounded. Garrett was the great nephew of Eugene Pate, the World War I veteran that the Eugene Pate American Legion Post is named for. Garrett was also very diligent about writing letters home from the war.

Evansville History Fact: In 1967 North High School wins the single-class basketball state championship.

David Eugene Gill

Military Information:

MOS: 11B40

Casualty Date: Thu. Sep. 2, 1965

Length of Tour: 73 Days

Grade: CPL/E4

Service: Army, Regular

Tour of Duty Began: 6/7/1965

Casualty Place: Province and Military Region Unknown, South Vietnam

On The Wall: Panel 02E, Line 073

Casualty Type: Hostile, Died, Air Loss, Crash, Helicopter-Crew

Personal Information:

Born: Tue. Oct. 28, 1941

Religion: Protestant, No Preference

Age at Casualty Date: 23

High School: North High School

Marital Status: Single

Race: Caucasian

Service Entry Point: Evansville, IN

Other Information: David Gill is considered the first casualty officially from Evansville. Leonard Lockard, who is listed on the backside of the Evansville memorial, was killed earlier but his service entry point was Pioneer, LA. Davis had also attended Howard Roosa Elementary School. Gill is buried in Jefferson Barracks Cemetery in St. Louis MO, which is where his mother resided at the time of his death.

Vietnam History Fact: On April 15, 1967 100,000 Vietnam War protesters gather in New York.

Richard H. Goheen

Military Information:

MOS: 62B20	Grade: SP4/E4
Casualty Date: Sat. Apr. 15, 1967	Service: Army, Regular
Length of Tour: 256 Days	Tour of Duty Began: 7/2/1966
	Casualty Place: Bien Hoa, South, Vietnam

On The Wall: Panel 18E, Line 029

Casualty Type: Hostile, Died, Misadventure, Ground Casualty

Personal Information:

Born: Wed. May 8, 1946	Marital Status: Single
Religion: Protestant, No Preference	Race: Caucasian
Age at Casualty Date: 20	Service Entry Point: Evansville, IN

High School: North High School, 1965 Grad.

Other Information: The military term misadventure refers mostly to accidental deaths. In this case a guard on duty mistakenly killed Goheen. In many of these "friendly fire" incidents a soldier would have wondered outside a guarded perimeter and been mistaken for an enemy soldier upon return to the perimeter.

Vietnam History Fact: By November 30, 1967 U.S. casualties reach 15,000.

Ronald Lee Groves

Military Information:

MOS: 11B20

Casualty Date: Tue. Feb 11, 1969

Length of Tour: 299 Days

Grade: SGT/E4

Service: Army, Selective Service

Tour of Duty Began: 4/20/1968

Casualty Place: Long Khanh, South Vietnam

On The Wall: Panel 32W, Line 012

Casualty Type: Hostile, Died, Gun, Small Arms Fire, Ground Casualty

Personal Information:

Born: Fri. June 18, 1948

Religion: Baptist, Other Groups

Age at Casualty Date: 20

High School: Central High School

Marital Status: Single

Race: Caucasian

Service Entry Point: Evansville, IN

Other Information: Ronald Groves had two sisters and a brother at the time of his death. His brother was a marine and was stationed in North Carolina at the time. Groves was also engaged and had planned to be married on July 5, 1969.

Vietnam History Fact: On January 30, 1968 Viet Cong guerillas launch the TET Offensive on South Vietnam. 268,000 Communist troops attack 105 Vietnamese cities and towns leaving 81,000 dead and 350,000 homeless.

David Emerson Hall

Military Information:

MOS: 3531

Casualty Date: Tue. Aug 16, 1966

Length of Tour: Cannot Determine

Grade: LCPL/E3

Service: Marine Corps, Regular

Tour of Duty Began: Not Reported

Casualty Place: Quang Tin, South Vietnam

On The Wall: Panel 10E, Line 013

Casualty Type: Hostile, Died, Other Explosive Device, Ground Casualty

Personal Information:

Born: Tue. Nov. 14, 1944

Religion: Protestant, No Preference

Age at Casualty Date: 21

High School: Bosse High School

Marital Status: Married

Race: Negro

Service Entry Point: Evansville, IN

Other Information: David Hall was killed while delivering ammunition near the fighting at Chu Lai. Hall had two sons, Gregory and David at the time of his death. He had been in the Marines since 1961. While the military had not reported his tour of duty start, a newspaper article reported he had been in Vietnam since January of 1966. According to a remembrance posted at the VVMF website Hall had taken the place of another soldier on the mission so Hall could see a friend. He is buried at Arlington National Cemetery.

Vietnam History Fact: On March 16, 1968 a U.S. Army platoon massacres men, women and children in the village My Lai.

Douglas Ray Harp

Military Information: Grade: PFC/E2
MOS: 0311 Service: Marine Corps, Regular
Casualty Date: Fri. Apr. 5, 1968 Tour of Duty Began: 11/29/1967
Length of Tour: 127 Days Casualty Place: Quang Tri, South Vietnam

On The Wall: Panel 48E, Line 017
Casualty Type: Hostile, Died, Gun, Small Arms Fire, Ground Casualty
Personal Information:
Born: Wed. Mar. 3, 1943 Marital Status: Married
Religion: Protestant, No Preference Race: Caucasian
Age at Casualty Date: 25 Service Entry Point: Evansville, IN
High School: Reitz High School

Other Information: Douglas Harp was an all-city tackle for the Reitz football team in 1961. Reitz won the city championship that year. The day before Harp was killed his wife received a letter stating he was looking forward to getting some rest on R & R in Hawaii.

Evansville History Fact: On June 22, 1968 the groundbreaking takes place for the campus of Indian State University Evansville.

Mark Thomas Heavrin

Military Information:	Grade: SGT/E4
MOS: 11B20	Service: Army, Selective Service
Casualty Date: Thu. Sep, 17, 1970	Tour of Duty Began: 10/15/1969
Length of Tour: 340 Days	Casualty Place: Quang Ngai, South Vietnam

On The Wall: Panel 07W, Line 070

Casualty Type: Hostile, Died, Other Explosive Device, Ground Casualty

Personal Information:

Born: Sun. June 12, 1949	Marital Status: Married
Religion: Roman Catholic	Race: Caucasian
Age at Casualty Date: 21	Service Entry Point: Evansville, IN

High School: Rex Mundi High School, 1967 Grad.

Other Information: Thomas Heavrin was due to come home in just three weeks. He was killed along with four other members of his platoon by a booby trap. Heavrin had a nine-month-old daughter whom he had seen on R & R in Hawaii in June. His friend from Evansville, Donald Kahre, was killed two days earlier in the same region.

Vietnam History Fact: On October 31, 1968 U.S. bombing of North Vietnam is halted.

Randall Allen Henze

Military Information:

MOS: 11B10

Casualty Date: Thu. Feb. 22, 1968

Length of Tour 77 Days

Grade: PFC/E3

Service: Army, Regular

Tour of Duty Began: 12/7/1967

Casualty Place: Thua Thien, South Vietnam

On The Wall: Panel 40E, Line 063

Casualty Type: Hostile, Died, Gun, Small Arms Fire, Ground Casualty

Personal Information:

Born: Wed. Apr. 21, 1943

Religion: Protestant, No Preference

Age at Casualty Date: 24

Marital Status: Single

Race: Caucasian

Service Entry Point: Evansville, IN

High School: Reitz High School, 1961 Grad.

Other Information: Randall Henze was also a graduate of Wabash College and was studying at McCormick Seminary in Chicago before leaving for Vietnam. Henze had a twin brother who was in graduate school at the University of Kentucky and another brother Richard who was a professor at the University of Kentucky. A remembrance posted at the VVMF website described Henze's death. Henze was a corpsman known as "Doc". He did not carry a weapon. Under enemy fire Henze went to some wounded soldiers to render aid. He did not wait for cover fire because they were moving their M 60 Machine gun and he thought it would take too long. As he was kneeling over one of the wounded soldiers he was mortally wounded. Henze was also an accomplished musician. He was a member of the all-city band while at Reitz High School.

Vietnam History Fact: By December of 1968 U.S. casualties reach 30,000.

David Lee Hollman

Military Information:

MOS: 0341

Casualty Date: Thu. Sep. 18, 1969

Length of Tour: 681 Days*

Grade: CPL/E4

Service: Marine Corps, Regular

Tour of Duty Began: 11/13/1967

Casualty Place: Quang Nam, South Vietnam

On The Wall: Panel 18W, Line 109

Casualty Type: Hostile, Died, Other Explosive Device, Ground Casualty

Personal Information:

Born: Tue. Feb. 22, 1949

Religion: Protestant, No Preference

Age at Casualty Date: 20

High School: Bosse High School

Marital Status: Single

Race: Caucasian

Service Entry Point: Evansville, IN

Other Information: * David Hollman was on his third tour in Vietnam. He had completed a one-year tour and a six month tour. His current tour was to last six months also. According to his grandmother he went back because of his friends and he felt sorry for how the Vietnamese lived. He felt like the soldiers were helping the Vietnamese people.

Vietnam History Fact: On January 16, 1969 peace talks begin between the Saigon government and the Viet Cong.

Clarence Ray Husk

Military Information:

MOS: 11E20

Casualty Date: Fri. May 12, 1967

Length of Tour: 225 Days

Grade: SGT/E5

Service: Army, Regular

Tour of Duty Began: 9/29/1966

Casualty Place: Binh Duong, South Vietnam

On The Wall: Panel 19E, line 096

Casualty Type: Hostile, Died, Gun, Small Arms Fire, Ground Casualty

Personal Information:

Born: Mon. Sep. 25, 1939

Religion: Baptist, Other Groups

Age at Casualty date: 27

High School: North High School

Marital Status: Married

Race: Caucasian

Service Entry Point: Evansville, IN

Other Information: Clarence Husk's wife was from Frankfort, Germany. He had two sons living with his wife in Germany at the time of his death. Husk is buried at Ft. Sam Houston National Cemetery in San Antonio, TX.

Vietnam History Fact: On March 16, 1969 the U.S. begins secret B-52 strikes in Cambodia.

Gerald Thomas Jenkins

Military Information:

MOS: 11B20

Casualty Date: Tue. Nov. 23, 1965

Length of Tour: 46 Days

On The Wall: Panel 10E, Line 013

Grade: Sp4/E4

Service: Army, Selective Service

Tour of Duty Began: 10/9/1965

Casualty Place: Province and Military Region Unknown, South Vietnam

Casualty Type: Hostile, Died, Multiple Fragmentation Wounds, Ground Casualty

Personal Information:

Born: Fri. May 5, 1944

Religion: Baptist, Other Groups

Age at Casualty Date: 21

High School: Central High School

Marital Status: Single

Race: Caucasian

Service Entry Point: Evansville, IN

Other Information: Jenkins had written a letter home four days before he was killed. His letter talked about capturing a Viet Cong guerilla and also seeing a dead enemy soldier. Most of his earlier letters did not mention much about the fighting. He did speak of how dense the jungle was and using machetes to cut their way through. Although the area where Jenkins was killed was not reported by the military according to a newspaper article he was killed near Plei Me.

Vietnam History Fact: On April 30, 1969 the U.S. troop strength peaked at 543,482 in country.

James Edward Jones

Military Information:

MOS: 67A1F	Grade: CPL/E3
	Service: Army, Regular
Casualty Date: Wed. Dec. 4, 1968	Tour of Duty Began, 3/8/1968
Length of Tour: 272 Days	Casualty Place: Binh Long, South Vietnam

On The Wall: Panel 37 W, Line 040

Casualty Type: Hostile, Died, Air Loss, Crash, Helicopter, Crew

Personal Information:

Born: Sun. Jan. 18, 1948	Marital Status: Single
Religion: Church of Christ	Race: Caucasian
Age at Casualty Date: 20	Service Entry Point: Evansville, IN

High School: Bosse High School, 1966 Grad.

Other Information: After three weeks into his assignment to an air assault battalion James Jones' helicopter was shot down. At first the crew was listed as MIA but seven days later the crew was found and identified. Jones had volunteered for the helicopter duty. Jones was on the football team at Bosse High School.

Vietnam History Fact: President Nixon announces Vietnamization on June 8, 1969. The plan is to withdraw 25,000 U.S. troops and replace them with South Vietnamese forces.

Donald Lee Kahre

Military Information:

MOS: 11B20

Casualty Date: Tue. Sep. 15, 1970

Length of Tour: 209 Days

Grade: SGT/E4

Service: Army, Selective Service

Tour of Duty Began: 2/19/1970

Casualty Place: Quang Ngai, South Vietnam

On The Wall: Panel 07W, Line 065

Casualty Type: Hostile, Died, Gun, Small Arms Fire, Ground Casualty

Personal Information:

Born: Sat. Sep 25, 1943

Religion: Lutheran & Missouri Synod

Age at Casualty Date: 26

High School: Unknown

Marital Status: Single

Race: Caucasian

Service Entry Point: Evansville, IN

Other Information: As mentioned earlier Kahre was killed two days before his friend Thomas Heavrin. Both had worked at Federal Produce before joining the service. Kahre had previously received the Purple Heart.

Vietnam History Fact: On July 30, 1969 President Nixon travels to Vietnam.

Gary Blaine Jones

Military Information:

MOS: 11B1P	Grade: PFC/E3
Casualty Date: Tue. Nov. 28, 1967	Service: Army, Regular
Length of Tour: 138 Days	Tour of Duty Began: 7/13/1967
	Casualty Place: Quang Tin, South Vietnam

On The Wall: Panel 30 E, Line 101

Casualty Type: Hostile, Died, Multiple Fragmentation Wounds, Ground Casualty

Personal Information:

Born: Thu. May 11, 1944	Marital Status: Married
Religion: Church of Christ	Race: Caucasian
Age at Casualty Date: 23	Service Entry Point: Evansville, IN

High School: North High School, 1962 Grad.

Other Information: Gary Jones was actually wounded on Oct. 3, 1967. He lost his left eye and was initially treated at a hospital in Vietnam. He was transferred to a hospital in Japan where he died of complications from his wounds. During his tour with the 101st Airborne Unit Jones saw most of his unit killed or wounded. He had also been assigned to search some tunnel complexes for weapon caches. He had mentioned in a letter he was never so scared. Jones was very active in his church, the Bellemeade Ave. Church of Christ.

Vietnam History Fact: On September 3, 1969 North Vietnamese leader Ho Chi Minh dies at the age of 79.

Michael Eugene Kraft

Military Information:

MOS: 1542

Casualty Date: Sat. Apr. 8, 1967

Length of Tour: 83 Days

Grade: 1 LT/02

Service: Army, Reserve

Tour of Duty Began: 1/15/1967

Casualty Place: Kinh Dihn, South Vietnam

On The Wall: Panel 17E, Line 124

Casualty Type: Hostile, Died While Missing, Gun, Small Arms Fire, Ground Casualty

Personal Information:

Born: Tue. Mar. 16 1943

Religion: Protestant, No Preference

Age at Casualty Date: 24

High School: Reitz High School

Marital Status: Married

Race: Caucasian

Service Entry Point: Evansville, IN

Other Information: The death of Michael Kraft prompted a local teacher, Ray Vescovi, to honor Kraft by naming a school award after him. The "Kraft Award" would go to a student each year that exemplified the qualities that Vescovi saw in Kraft. According to Vescovi, Kraft was a great athlete, student and competitor along with being a gentleman. The first award went to student Bruce Lipper, an eight grader at Cynthia Heights Elementary School. Kraft had a 5-month-old son at the time of his death. He attended Indian University before going into the service and entering officers training at Ft. Benning, Georgia.

Vietnam History Fact: On October 15, 1969 millions across the U.S. participate in the Moratorium, the largest one-day demonstration against the war.

Thomas Roger Keppen

Military Information:	Grade: 1 LT/02
MOS: 0302	Service: Marine Corps, Reserve
Casualty Date: Sun. July 7, 1968	Tour of Duty Began: 12/3/1967
Length Of Tour: 216 Days	Casualty Place: Quang Tri, South Vietnam

On The Wall: Panel 53W, Line 036

Casualty Type: Hostile, Died, Artillery, Mortar, Rocket, Ground Casualty

Personal Information:

Born: Sat. Oct. 27, 1945	Marital Status: Single
Religion: Roman Catholic	Race: Caucasian
Age at Casualty Date: 22	Service Entry Point: Evansville, IN
High School: Memorial High School	

Other Information: Thomas Keppen was scheduled to go on R & R July 19 in Australia according to a letter he had sent his parents. On the same day they received the letter they were informed by telegram that Keppen had been killed. Keppen was a standout baseball catcher for Memorial High School and later Evansville College where he completed a degree in secondary education. He had planned on a teaching career after completing military duty.

Vietnam History Fact: On May 4, 1970 four students at Kent State in Ohio are killed by National Guardsmen during a violent antiwar demonstration on campus.

John Oscar Kerney

Military Information:	Grade: PFC/E2
MOS: 0311	Service: Marine Corps, Regular
Casualty Date: Wed. Sep. 13, 1967	Tour of Duty Began: Not Reported
Length Of Tour: Cannot Determine	Casualty Place: Quang Nam, South Vietnam

On The Wall: Panel 26E, Line 066

Casualty Type: Hostile, Died, Multiple Fragmentation Wounds, Ground Casualty

Personal Information:

Born: Wed. Sep. 24, 1947	Marital Status: Single
Religion: Protestant, No Preference	Race: Caucasian
Age at Casualty date: 19	Service Entry Point: Evansville, IN

High School: Bosse High School, 1965 Grad.

Other Information: Although Kerney's tour of duty start was not reported by the military a newspaper article reported he left for Vietnam on May 19, 1967. Kerney had spent some time at Indiana State University Evansville before enlisting in the Marines.

Evansville History Fact: In 1970 the Evansville Triplets were established as a Triple AAA baseball team; one step below the major leagues.

Thomas Michael Koch

Military Information:	Grade: PFC/E3
MOS 11B10	Service: Army, Selective Service
Casualty Date: Sat. May 28, 1966	Tour of Duty Began: 1/1/1966
Length of Tour: 147 Days	Casualty Place: Province and Military Region Unknown
On The Wall: Panel 073, Line 113	South Vietnam

Casualty Type: Hostile, Died, Multiple Fragmentation Wounds, Ground Casualty

Personal Information:

Born: Fri. Feb. 18, 1944	Marital Status; Single
Religion: Roman Catholic	Race: Caucasian
Age at Casualty date: 22	Service Entry Point: Evansville, IN

High School: Rex Mundi High School, 1962 Grad.

Other Information: Thomas Koch had three brothers, Raymond, Robert, and James. Raymond also served in Vietnam.

Vietnam History Fact: On June 24, 1970 the U.S. Senate votes overwhelmingly to repeal the Gulf of Tonkin Resolution.

Thomas Leo McBride

Military Information:

MOS: 0331

Casualty Date: Wed. June 5, 1968

Length of Tour: 95 Days

Grade: LCPL/E3

Service: Marine Corps, Regular

Tour of Duty Began: 2/28/1968

Casualty Place: Quang Nam, South Vietnam

On The Wall: Panel 60W, Line 024

Casualty Type: Hostile, Died, Gun, Small Arms Fire, Ground Casualty

Personal Information:

Born: Sat. Nov. 12, 1949

Religion: Roman Catholic

Age at Date of Casualty: 18

High School: Mater Dei High School

Marital Status: Single

Race: Caucasian

Service Entry Point: Evansville, IN

Other Information: McBride was the only KIA from Mater Dei High School that occurred during the Vietnam War. A memorial tree was planted there in honor of McBride. A teacher and friend of mine, Mike Goebel, at Mater Dei teaches an extensive unit on the Vietnam War. He has the students read "A Rumor of War" by Phillip Caputo as part of the unit.

Evansville History Fact: In 1971 the University of Evansville won its fifth NCAA Division II championship in basketball.

Charles Albert McDaniels

Military Information:

MOS: 11C10	Grade: PFC/E3
	Service: Army, Regular
Casualty Date: Mon. Mar. 20, 1967	Tour of Duty Began: 9/19/1966
Length of Tour: 213 Days	Casualty Place: Kinh Dinh, South Vietnam

On The Wall: Panel 16E, Line 125

Casualty Type: Hostile, Died, Gun, Small Arms Fire, Ground Casualty

Personal Information:

Born: Wed. June 19, 1946	Marital Status: Single
Religion: Roman Catholic	Race: Caucasian
Age at Casualty Date: 20	Service Entry Point: Evansville, IN
High School: Unknown	

Other Information: I was unable to find any more information on Charles McDaniels.

Vietnam History Fact: On February 8, 1971 South Vietnamese forces begin attacks on the Ho Chi Minh Trail in Laos.

Bruce Edward Mielke

Military Information:

MOS: 0341

Casualty Date: Tue. Aug. 1, 1967

Length of Tour: Cannot Determine

Grade: LCPL/E3

Service: Marine Corps, Regular

Tour of Duty Began: Not Reported

Casualty Place: Quang Tin, South Vietnam

On The Wall: Panel 24E, Line 062

Casualty Type: Hostile, Died, Gun, Small Arms Fire, Ground Casualty

Personal Information:

Born: Mon. Mar. 8, 1948

Religion: Protestant, No Preference

Age at Casualty Date: 19

High School: Central High School

Marital Status: Single

Race: Caucasian

Service Entry Point: Evansville, IN

Other Information: Bruce Mielke was the friend of William "Stan" Daugherty who was also killed in Vietnam. As stated earlier they attended Central High School together. They shared athletic interests and spent much time together. In November of 1967 students at Columbia School in Evansville planted a Dogwood tree in honor of Mielke who had attended school there as an elementary student.

Vietnam History Fact: On March 29, 1971 Lt. William Calley is convicted by an Army court martial for his part in the My Lai massacre.

George Monroe Moore

Military Information

MOS: 31G40

Casualty Date: Jan. 23, 1968

Length of Tour: 276 Days

On The Wall: Panel 35E, Line: 019

Grade: SFC/E6

Service: Army, Regular

Tour of Duty Began: 4/22/1967

Casualty Place: Province and Military Region Unknown, South Vietnam

Casualty Type: Non-hostile, Illness/disease, Ground Casualty

Personal Information:

Born: July 28, 1924

Religion: Baptist–Other Groups

Age at Casualty Date: 44

High School: Unknown

Marital Status: Single

Race: Caucasian

Service Entry Point: Evansville, IN

Other Information: I was unable to find any other information about Moore.

Evansville History Fact: In 1971 Central High School moves to its present location on First Avenue.

William Junior Moore

Military Information:

MOS: 0351

Casualty Date: Sat. May 25, 1968

Length of Tour: 58 Days

Grade: PFC/E2

Service: Marine Corps, Regular

Tour of Duty Began: 4/5/1968

Casualty Place: Quang Tri, South Vietnam

On The Wall: Panel 67W, Line 002

Casualty Type: Hostile, Died, Gun, Small Arms Fire, Ground Casualty

Personal Information:

Born: Thu. Aug. 11, 1949

Religion: Roman Catholic

Age at Casualty date: 18

High School: North High School

Marital Status: Single

Race: Caucasian

Service Entry Point: Evansville, IN

Other Information: William Moore had been chosen as "Mr. North" for his outstanding weightlifting ability while in high school. He was also a member of the football team. Three days before his death his family received a letter from Moore complaining about how the war was going. He was killed while on a combat mission that at this point in the war was called search & destroy. Quang Tri Province was especially dangerous as it was very close to the demilitarized zone and had heavy concentrations of enemy soldiers.

Evansville History Fact: In 1971 The Reitz High School football team goes 10–0.

Charles Doyle Oglesby

Military Information:

MOS: 11C20

Casualty Date: Mon. Apr. 11, 1966

Length of Tour: 263 Days

On The Wall: Panel 06E, Line 103

Grade: SP4/E4

Service: Army, Regular

Tour of Duty Began: 7/22/1965

Casualty Place: Province and Military Region Unknown South Vietnam

Casualty Type: Hostile, Died, Multiple Fragmentation Wounds, Ground Casualty

Personal Information:

Born: Sun. Jan. 2, 1944

Religion: Protestant, No Preference

Age at Casualty Date: 22

High School: North High School

Marital Status: Single

Race: Caucasian

Service Entry Point; Evansville, IN

Other Information: The pallbearers for Charles Oglesby's funeral were soldiers from Ft. Benjamin Harrison.

Evansville History Fact: In 1972 Russell Lloyd Sr. becomes mayor after 12 years of service by Frank McDonald.

Kerry Wayne Phillips

Military Information:	Grade: SGT/E5
MOS: 12B40	Service: Army, Regular
Casualty Date: Sat. Dec. 19, 1970	Tour of Duty Began: 2/15/1970
Length of Tour: 308 Days	Casualty Place: Province and Military Region Unknown
On The Wall: Panel 06W, Line 133	South Vietnam

Casualty Type: Hostile, Died, Gun, Small Arms Fire, Ground Casualty

Personal Information:

Born: Sat. Oct 6, 1951	Marital Status: Single
Religion: Presbyterian	Race: Caucasian
Age at Casualty Date: 19	Service Entry Point: Evansville, IN
High School: Central High School	

Other Information: Kerry Phillips was due to go on leave in January when he was killed. He had signed up for an eight-month extension because he really liked the Vietnamese people. According to a letter he would have liked to finish his military duty and return to Vietnam in a civilian capacity. While helping me research this project one of my middle school students recognized Phillips as her uncle. She was actually named after him. When we rededicated the Evansville memorial my student read her uncles name along with some of the other Evansville casualties as part of the ceremony. All of the names were read and students that would be attending the high schools of the casualties were chosen to read them. Although the region Phillips was killed was not reported his unit was based at Quan Loi. He was with an engineering unit that did road construction. They were attacked by enemy forces while en-route to a road project.

Evansville History Fact: In 1972 Rex Mundi High School closes leaving Evansville with two Catholic High Schools. Five Rex Mundi graduates died in Vietnam.

Emory Lee Rea

Military Information:

MOS: 11B20

Casualty Date: Thu. Dec. 4, 1969

Length of Tour: 199 Days

Grade: SP4/E4

Service: Army, Selective Service

Tour of Duty Began: 5/20/1969

Casualty Place: Long An, South Vietnam

On The Wall: Panel 09W, Line 048

Casualty Type: Hostile, Died, Other Explosive Device, Ground Casualty

Personal Information:

Born: Thu. Nov. 28, 1946

Religion: Methodist

Age at Casualty Date: 23

Marital Status: Single

Race: Caucasian

Service Entry Point: Evansville, IN

High School: Bosse High School, 1964 Grad.

Other Information: Emory Rea was also a graduate of Indiana University with a major in Zoology. He spent a lot of time in what was called at the time Stockwell Woods, which would later become Wesselman's Nature Preserve. Rea was one of the first to have an idea for a nature center at the park. He had written a journal entry as a youth about his idea. In his honor friends and family donated $634 to a fund for construction of a building to be used as an interpretive center for the 200-acre nature preserve. Later Rea's mother donated another $200, which was part of Rea's last pay from the military. Rea also received nine posthumous awards for his service including the bronze star with two oak leaf clusters. In a posted remembrance on the VVMF website a college friend talked at length about Rea and mentioned that they drove from Indiana University to Pasadena, CA to watch IU in the Rose Bowl.

Vietnam History Fact: On March 30, 1972 North Vietnam launched an Easter Offensive on South Vietnam.

Donald Ray Rhodes

Military Information:

MOS: 11B40

Casualty Date: Thu. Feb. 27, 1969

Length of Tour: 289 Days

Grade: SGT/E5

Service: Army, Regular

Tour of Duty Began: 5/14/1968

Casualty Place: Gia Dinh, South Vietnam

On The Wall: Panel 31W, Line 084

Casualty Type: Hostile, Died, Burns, Ground Casualty

Personal Information:

Born: Mon. Aug. 3, 1942

Religion: Baptist, Other Groups

Age at Casualty Date: 26

High School: Bosse High School

Marital Status: Married

Race: Caucasian

Service Entry Point: Evansville, IN

Other Information: A remembrance was posted at the VVMF website by Rhodes' younger brother thanking him for letting him drive the car home one day and telling his mother what a good job he did. Rhodes was also posthumously awarded the Distinguished Service Cross.

Vietnam History Fact: On Dec. 29, 1972 President Nixon halts bombing in Vietnam.

Danny Ray Schmidt

Military Information:

MOS: 11B2V

Casualty Date: Fri. June 12, 1970

Length of Tour: 210 Days

Grade: SP4/E4

Service: Army, Selective Service

Tour of Duty Began: 11/17/1969

Casualty Place: Unknown Code, Cambodia

On The Wall: Panel 09W, Line 048

Casualty Type: Hostile, Died, Gun, Small Arms Fire, Ground Casualty

Personal Information:

Born: Fri. July 8, 1949

Religion: Protestant, No Preference

Age at Casualty Date: 20

High School: North High School

Marital Status: Single

Race: Caucasian

Service Entry Point: Evansville, IN

Other Information: Schmidt was planning to be married in July in Hawaii. Schmidt was the first Evansville soldier to be officially listed as killed in Cambodia. He had written a letter home about how much he loved his country but did not like what the U.S. was doing with this war. Schmidt had five brothers and three sisters at the time of his death.

Vietnam History Fact: On January 27, 1973 the Vietnam Peace Treaty is signed in Paris.

Kenneth Eugene Slater

Military Information:

Grade: PFC/E3

MOS: 11H10

Service: Army, Regular

Casualty Date: Wed. Nov. 1, 1967

Tour of Duty Began: 9/22/1967

Length of Tour: 40 Days

Casualty Place: Tay Ninh, South Vietnam

On The Wall: Panel 29E, Line 006

Casualty Type: Hostile, Died, Gun, Small Arms Fire, Ground Casualty

Personal Information:

Born: Mon. June 20, 1949

Marital Status: Married

Religion: Lutheran & Missouri Synod

Race: Caucasian

Age at Casualty Date: 19

Service Entry Point: Evansville, IN

High School: Reitz High School

Other Information: Slater had a five-month-old daughter at the time of his death. A cousin of Slater's described their relationship more like that of brothers on the VVMF website. His cousin has left several postings about Slater's nieces.

Evansville History Fact: On January 29, 1973, just two days after the signing of the peace treaty, the Evansville memorial is dedicated making it probably the first Vietnam War Memorial in the country.

Larry Paul Stotler

Military Information:

MOS: 1204

Casualty Date: Mon. Oct. 16, 1967

Length of Tour: 249 Days

Grade: Capt/03

Service: Army, Reserve

Tour of Duty Began: 2/9/1967

Casualty Place: Kinh Dinh, South Vietnam

On The Wall: Panel 28E, Line 017

Casualty Type: Hostile, Died, Other Explosive Device, Ground Casualty

Personal Information:

Born: Tue. Nov. 4, 1941

Religion: Baptist, Other Groups

Age at Casualty Date: 25

Marital Status: Married

Race: Caucasian

Service Entry Point: Evansville, IN

High School: Bosse High School, 1959 Grad.

Other Information: Larry Stotler had 3 children at the time of his death. A seven-year-old son and two daughters age five and three. Stotler was killed when the jeep he was riding in ran over a landmine. Stotler played football for Bosse High School.

Vietnam History Fact: On March 29, 1973 the last American combat troops leave Vietnam.

Randall Alan Thompson

Military Information:

MOS. 11B10

Casualty Date: Thu. Mar. 25, 1971

Length of Tour: 76 Days

Grade: CPL/E3

Service: Army, Selective Service

Tour of Duty Began 1/9/1971

Casualty Place: Quang Tri, South Vietnam

On The Wall: Panel 04W, Line 078

Casualty Type: Hostile, Died while missing, Gun, Small Arms Fire, ground Casualty

Personal Information:

Born: Fri. July 7, 1950

Religion: Protestant, No Preference

Age at Casualty Date: 20

High School: Harrison High School

Marital Status: Single

Race: Caucasian

Service Entry Point: Evansville, IN

Other Information: Thompson was enrolled at Indiana State University Evansville when he was drafted. Thompson was part of a unit that was supporting the South Vietnamese in Laos when he was killed. He had been reported missing when his unit came under heavy fire. His unit was featured earlier on a news program when fifty-two men refused an order to retrieve military equipment while under heavy enemy fire. None of the men were disciplined but the commanding officer was. A fellow teacher and friend of mine, Rob Spear, was a friend of Thompson.

Vietnam History Fact: On June 22, 1974 the Vietnamese reconciliation talks break down. By this date 18,000 South Vietnamese and 66,000 North Vietnamese have been killed since the signing of the peace treaty.

Raymond Anthony Wagner

Military Information:

MOS: Not Reported

Casualty Date: Mon. Mar 27, 1972

Length of Tour: 1 Day*

Grade: A1C/E3

Service: Air Force, Regular

Tour of Duty Began: 3/27/1972

Casualty Place: Unknown Code, Cambodia

On The Wall: Panel 02W, Line 120

Casualty Type: Hostile, Died While Missing, Air Loss, Crash, Helicopter-Crew

Personal Information:

Born: Mon. Oct.22, 1951

Religion: No Preference

Age at Casualty Date: 20

Marital Status: Single

Race: Caucasian

Service Entry Point: Evansville, IN

High School: Rex Mundi, 1969 Grad.

Other Information: Wagner had been in Southeast Asia a little over three months. He was based in Thailand, which accounts for his 1 day tour. How much time he actually spent in hostile territory is unknown. Wagner was trained in Para-rescue and was on a rescue mission when their helicopter crashed. Wagner had been a member of the wrestling team at Rex Mundi High School. He was engaged to be married upon return from military duty.

Vietnam History Fact: On April 23, 1975 President Gerald Ford speaking in New Orleans calls the Vietnam War finished.

Wayne Alan Wilcox

Military Information:	Grade: SGT/E4
MOS: 11B20	Service: Army, Regular
Casualty Date: Sat. Feb. 15, 1969	Tour of Duty Began: 5/10/1968
Length of Tour: 281 Days	Casualty Place: Long An, South Vietnam

On The Wall: Panel 32W, Line 041

Casualty Type: Hostile, Died, Burns, Ground Casualty

Personal Information:

Born: Mon. Oct. 25, 1948	Marital Status: Single
Religion: Roman Catholic	Race: Caucasian
Age at Casualty Date: 20	Service Entry Point: Evansville

High School: Harrison High School

Other Information: Wayne Wilcox had three brothers and six sisters at the time of his death. A posting at the VVMF website gives a detailed description of the battle in which Wilcox was killed. The fellow soldier that posted the story commented what a great soldier Wilcox was. He stated that Wilcox was the first one to come to his aid when he was wounded in the field. He said you could always count on Wayne. Wilcox served with $2^{nd}/147^{th}$ Mechanized Infantry. Wilcox was one of 195 soldiers of that unit that died and the survivors established a memorial scholarship to honor the memory of those men.

Vietnam History Fact: On April 29, 1975 the U.S. Embassy in Saigon was evacuated and all U.S. personnel were out of Vietnam.

Donald Maurice Wilson

Military Information:

MOS: 71193

Casualty Date: Fri. Aug.4, 1967

Length of Tour: 10 Days

Grade: 1 LT/02

Service: Army, Reserve

Tour of Duty Began: 7/26/1967

Casualty Place: Quang Ngai, South Vietnam

On The Wall: Panel 24E, Line 079

Casualty Type: Hostile, Died, Other Explosive Device, Ground Casualty

Personal Information:

Born: Tue. July 11, 1939

Religion: Protestant, No Preference

Age at Casualty Date: 28

Marital Status: Married

Race: Caucasian

Service Entry Point: Evansville, IN

High School: Newcomerstown High School, Ohio, 1957 Grad.

Other Information: Donald Wilson met his wife, a former Central High student, while at Ft. Campbell. He had three children, 2 daughters and a son, at the time of his death.

Vietnam History Fact: On April 30, 1975 Saigon falls to the North Vietnamese forces.

"The Other Side"

The plaque added to the backside of the memorial was added because originally two names had been omitted from a department of defense document. Ten other soldiers with Evansville or Vanderburgh County connections were also added. A controversy arose from the fact the original idea for the memorial was to honor those soldiers who were officially from Vanderburgh County. This can become confusing because the military lists a soldier's hometown based on where they enlisted not necessarily what is truly their hometown.

There also may have been some contention because two of the names added are not considered casualties of the Vietnam War. I have not personally heard any of these complaints from anyone that feels that way but was told by some veterans that there were some who disapproved of these names being added. Since the purpose of this book is to honor the soldiers listed on this memorial I felt the need to include all those listed.

Another controversy about the memorial is that after a certain time some began to question the adequacy of this memorial considering the tremendous amount of sacrifice that is represented by so many lives lost. I guess because of the unpopularity of the war and the pain associated with the terrible treatment of some returning soldiers these issues were not addressed. On Veterans Day, November 11, 2007 a new memorial was dedicated in Evansville. It consists of 2 black marble panels set at the same angle as the Memorial Wall in Washington D.C. Sixty-five of the sixty-seven names on the original memorial are listed. The names of Thomas Bitter and Ken Bowman are not listed because they are not officially Vietnam War casualties.

Evansville owes a great deal of thanks to Mark Acker and the VFW Post 1114 for their hard work in making this new memorial a reality.

Casualty Profiles—The Other Side

Larry Hutton Bowers

Military Information:

MOS: 11B20

Casualty Date: Fri. Dec. 8, 1967

Length of Tour: 204 Days

Grade: SP4/E4

Service: Army, Selective Service

Tour of Duty Began: 5/18/1967

Casualty Place: Quang Nam, South Vietnam

On The Wall: Panel 31E, Line 063

Casualty Type: Hostile, Died, Other Explosive Device, Ground Casualty

Personal Information:

Born: Sat. Nov. 9, 1946

Religion: Baptist, Other Groups

Age at casualty Date: 21

Marital Status: Married

Race: Caucasian

Service Entry Point: Evansville, IN

Hugh School: Harrison High School, 1965 Grad.

Other Information: Bowers was married five days before he left for Vietnam. Bowers is the first soldier listed on the backside of the memorial.

Vietnam History Fact: By December 1975 more than 1.5 million Vietnamese have left the country for a "safe haven."

Jack Allen Bowman

Military Information:	Grade: PFC/E2
MOS: 0351	Service: Marine Corps, Regular
Casualty Date: Sun. Nov.17, 1968	Tour of Duty Began: 8/17/1968
Length of Tour: 92 Days	Casualty Place: Quang Nam, South Vietnam

On The Wall: Panel 39W, Line 077

Casualty Type: Hostile, Died, Gun, Small Arms Fire, Ground Casualty

Personal Information:

Born: Sun. Sep 25, 1949	Marital Status: Single
Religion: Protestant, No Preference	Race: Caucasian
Age at Casualty Date: 19	Service Entry Point: Evansville, IN

High School: Central High School

Other Information: Bowman was one of the two that was omitted from the original list of soldiers from Vanderburgh County that prompted a plaque on the backside of the memorial. Bowman was the other soldier that had a relative that was in a history class at my school. His nephew assisted with the original research that we did as part of our history class. Bowman was an uncle on the student's father's side of the family.

Vietnam History Fact: On July 2, 1976 North and South Vietnam are officially reunited.

Prentice Fay Brenton

Military Information:

Grade: SSGT/E5

MOS: Not Reported

Service: Air Force, Regular

Casualty Date: Thu. Mar. 9, 1967

Tour of Duty Began: 7/6/1966

Length of Tour: 246 Days

Casualty Place: Quang Ngai, South Vietnam

On The Wall: Panel 16E, Line 043

Casualty Type: Hostile, Died While Missing, Air Loss, Crash, Fixed Wing-Crew

Personal Information:

Born: Wed. Mar 10, 1926

Marital Status: Married

Religion: Other, Not Reported

Race: Caucasian

Age at Casualty Date: 40

Service Entry Point: Spokane, WA

High School: Unknown

Other Information: Brenton's mother resided in Evansville at the time of his death. Brenton was career military. He was in the Marines for eight years and was in the Air Force for 10 years before his death. He also served in World War II and Korea. Brenton was killed while flying an unarmed reconnaissance mission aboard the EC-47. Brenton received a total of thirteen service medals and commendations during his military career.

Vietnam History Fact: On September 20, 1977 Vietnam is admitted to the United Nations.

Thomas Joseph Bitter

Military Information:

MOS: Seaman Apprentice	Grade: Unknown
	Service: Navy, Regular
Casualty Date: July 30, 1968	Tour of Duty Began: Aug. 1965
Length of Tour: Cannot Determine	Casualty Place: Alameda, CA harbor

Casualty Type: Accident aboard USS Coral Sea

Personal Information:

Born: Unknown	Marital Status: Married
Religion: Roman Catholic	Race: Caucasian
Age at Casualty Date: 23	Service Entry Point: Evansville, IN

High School: North High School, 1965 Grad

Other Information: Thomas Bitter is not an official Vietnam War casualty because he was not killed in the Vietnam theater even though he had already served two tours in the Gulf of Tonkin aboard the USS Coral Sea. Bitter's father, Carl, was a friend of mine that I met through the Evansville Handball Club. His father was responsible for getting two sets of outdoor handball courts built in Evansville. I began playing the game in high school and continued as an adult and consequently met Carl. It turned out that my grandfather was a friend of Carl's also. Carl passed away on April 29, 1991. What turned out to be interesting is that all the time I knew Carl I had no idea he had a son. I discovered his son's name during my initial research of the memorial in 2002. I guess he just did not want to talk about it.

Vietnam History Fact: During 1978 thousands leave Southeast Asia, including those known as the "Boat People."

Lloyd Patterson Hyde

Military Information:

MOS: 2105

Casualty Date: Wed. Oct. 26, 1966

Length of Tour: Cannot Determine

Grade: LT/O3

Service: Navy, Reserve

Tour of Duty Began: Not Reported

Casualty Place: Unknown Code, North Vietnam

On The Wall: Panel 11E, Line111

Casualty Type: Non-Hostile, Died, Other Causes, Sea Casualty

Personal Information:

Born: Sat. Mar. 19, 1938

Religion: Protestant, No Preference

Age at Casualty Date: 28

High School: Unknown

Marital Status: Married

Race: Caucasian

Service Entry Point: Atlanta, GA

Other Information: Lloyd Hyde served aboard the USS Oriskany. He was a graduate of the Indiana University School of Medicine. A fire aboard the ship led to the death of Hyde.

Vietnam History Fact: On March 23, 1978 the Vietnamese government nationalizes privately owned businesses in Saigon.

Leonard Wayne Lockard

Military Information:

MOS: 62D220

Casualty Date: Fri. July 10, 1964

Length of Tour: Cannot Determine

On The Wall: Panel 01E, Line 057

Grade: SP5/E5

Service: Army, Regular

Tour of Duty Began: Not Reported

Casualty Place: Province and Military region Unknown, South Vietnam

Casualty Type: Hostile, Died, Air Loss, Crash, Helicopter,-Crew

Personal Information:

Born: Thu. July 20, 1944

Religion: Roman Catholic

Age at Casualty Date: 19

High School: Unknown

Marital Status: Married

Race: Caucasian

Service Entry Point: Pioneer, LA

Other Information: Leonard Lockard was serving as door gunner on a helicopter in support of South Vietnamese forces fighting the Viet Cong. He was the 250th U.S. serviceman and first from Evansville to die in Vietnam. According to a newspaper article Lockard planned to make the military a career. He received the Distinguished Flying Cross posthumously. Lockard had a six-day-old son the day he was killed.

Vietnam History Fact: On November 13, 1982 the Vietnam Veterans Memorial is dedicated.

Thomas Curtis Metsker

Military Information:	Grade: CAPT/O3
MOS: 1542	Service: Army, Reserve
Casualty Date: Sun: Nov. 14, 1965	Tour of Duty Began: 8/6/1965
Length of Tour: 81 Days	Casualty Place: Province and Military Region Unknown, South Vietnam
On The Wall: Panel 03E, Line 049	

Casualty Type: Hostile, Died, Gun, Small Arms Fire, Ground Casualty

Personal Information:

Born: Sat. May 20, 1939	Marital Status: Married
Religion: Protestant, No Preference	Race: Caucasian
Age at Casualty Date: 26	Service Entry Point: Indianapolis, IN
High School: Unknown	

Other Information: Tom Metsker became somewhat famous when his story was told in the book" We were soldiers once.... and Young" by Joe Galloway and Colonel Harold G. Moore. The incident in which he was killed is a scene in the movie that was derived from the book. Metsker's connection to Evansville stems from his wife who lived in Newburgh, IN with their seventeen-month-old daughter. Metsker's daughter eventually went on to Harrison High School where she had a locker next to my brother's. They graduated in the same class. Metsker was also a graduate of The Citadel.

Because of my affiliation with VVMF I was able to meet Joe Galloway. He was the only war correspondent at the Battle of the Ia Drang Valley where Metsker was killed. Due to the intensity of the battle Galloway was forced out of his role as a reporter and took up arms. He received the highest military honor that can be earned by a civilian. Galloway was also part of the delegation I traveled with to Vietnam in April of 2005. There are several remembrance postings to Metsker at the VVMF website.

Vietnam History Fact: From July 17-21, 2002 the Vietnam Veterans Memorial Fund conducted its first Teach Vietnam Teachers' Conference in Washington D.C.

Michael Lee Miller

Military Information:

MOS: 11C10

Casualty Date: Oct. 3/1967

Length of Tour: 186 Days

On The Wall: Panel 27E, Line 45

Grade: PFC/E3

Service: Army, Selective Service

Tour of Duty Began: 4/1/1967

Casualty Place: Province and Military Region Unbknown, South Vietnam

Casualty Type: Hostile, Died, Multiple Fragmentation Wounds, Ground Casualty

Personal Information:

Born: Aug. 22, 1947

Religion: Baptist, Other Groups

Age at Casualty Date: 20

High School: Bosse High School

Marital Status: Single

Race: Caucasian

Service Entry Point: Henderson, KY

Other Information: Michael Miller's family move to Henderson, KY after he graduated from Bosse. He was wounded in August and spent time in a Vietnamese hospital in critical condition until the time of his death. He wrote letters home with the assistance of a nurse before he died.

Vietnam History Fact: On April 7, 2003 the Evansville Vietnam War Memorial is rededicated, commemorating the 30th anniversary of the original dedication.

Dallas Henry Moore

Military Information:

MOS: Not Reported

Casualty Date: Wed., Mar. 6, 1968

Length of Tour: 106 Days

Grade: SGT/E4

Service: Air Force, Regular

Tour of Duty Began: 11/21/1967

Casualty Place: Quang Tri, South Vietnam

On The Wall: Panel 43E, Line 027

Casualty Type Hostile, Died While Missing, Air Loss, Crash, Fixed Wing-Crew

Personal Information:

Born: Sun. Oct. 6, 1940

Religion: Baptist, Other Groups

Age at Casualty Date: 27

High School: Unknown

Marital Status: Married

Race: Caucasian

Service Entry Point: Headland, AL

Other Information: According to a newspaper article Dallas Moore received the Distinguished Flying Cross, Air Medal, Silver Star, and Purple Heart posthumously. Moore was a flight engineer aboard a C-123 that was flying support missions to Khe Sanh. Moore had a young daughter at the time of his death.

Vietnam History Fact: From April 22–May 1, 2005 a delegation of educators, veterans, and architects designing the new education center for the Vietnam Memorial travel to Vietnam to tour the country and raise awareness for Project Renew. The delegation also observed Vietnam's 30th anniversary commemoration of the end of the war in Ho Chi Minh City (Saigon).

Gerald W. Nicholson, Jr.

Military Information:

MOS: 6321

Casualty Date: Sat. Nov. 1, 1969

Length of Tour: 92 Days

Grade: LCPL/E3

Service: Marine Corps, Regular

Tour of Duty Began: 8/2/1969

Casualty Place: Quang Nam, South Vietnam

On The Wall: Panel 16W, Line 014

Casualty Type: Non-hostile, Died, Other Causes, Air Loss, Crash, Helicopter-Crew

Personal Information:

Born: Mon. Oct. 2, 1950

Religion: Protestant, No Preference

Age at Casualty Date: 19

High School: Unknown

Marital Status: Single

Race: Caucasian

Service Entry Point: Hialeah, FL

Other Information: Gerald Nicholson was killed when the engine of the helicopter in which he was riding exploded. Nicholson's family had left Evansville when he was seven years old. Nicholson's father had died in a plane crash on Grand Bahama Island in 1964.

Quote: "There never was a good war or a bad peace"-Benjamin Franklin

Richard Allen Noelke

Military Information:

MOS: 11B20

Casualty Date: Sat. Nov. 6, 1965

Length of Tour: 87 Days

On The Wall: Panel 03E, Line 026

Grade: PFC/E3

Service: Army, Regular

Tour of Duty Began: 8/20/1965

Casualty Place: Province and Military region Unknown, South Vietnam

Casualty Type: Hostile, Died, Gun, Small Arms Fire, Ground Casualty

Personal Information:

Born: Mon. Feb. 7, 1944

Religion: Roman Catholic

Age at Casualty Date: 21

Marital Status: Single

Race: Caucasian

Service Entry Point: Fontana, CA

High School, Rex Mundi High School

Other Information: Richard Noelke was presented the Silver Star posthumously. It was stated he was responsible for saving several lives. He was killed while giving aid to a fellow platoon member. Noelke was a medic. Another good friend of mine I met through our handball club, Tom Chappell, was a good friend of Noelke's growing up. They went to Rex Mundi High school together. Chappell also served in Vietnam from 1966–1967. They were at Rex Mundi at the same time as one of our most famous natives, Bob Griese.

Quote: "Anyone, who truly wants to go to war, has truly never been there."– Larry Reeves

Thomas W. Reasor

Military Information:

MOS: Pilot

Casualty Date: July 30, 1972

Length of Tour: Cannot Determine

On The Wall: Panel 1W, Line 61

Grade: CAPT/O3

Service: Air Force, Regular

Tour of Duty Began: Unknown

Casualty Place: Province and Military Region Unknown, Thailand

Casualty Type: Non-hostile, Died, Air Loss, Crash, Fixed Wing-Crew

Personal Information:

Born: Feb. 19, 1944

Religion: Unknown

Age at Casualty Date: 28

High School: Reitz High School, 1962 Grad.

Marital Status: Married

Race: Caucasian

Service Entry Point: Evansville, IN

Other Information: Reasor was the pilot of a B-52 when it was damaged in a thunderstorm and crashed. Reasor was an all-city football player and co-captain of the Reitz football team. Reasor attended the Air Force Academy for one year and then transferred to the Evansville College where he graduated in 1966. Reaasor had a three and a half year old son and a two and half month old son at the time of his death. His family resided in California but was in Evansville visiting Reasor's parents when he was killed. Reasor was the second of two left off the casualty list that prompted the addition of the plaque to the backside of the memorial.

Quote: " I guess that's the great sadness to war, the plants, the flowers, the trees all grow back, but people don't"–Dennis Mannion (A Walk in the Clouds).

Evansville's Vietnam Casualties by High School

Benjamin Bosse High School
  Stephen Bruce Boehne
  James Wisdom Bowling
  William Stanley Daugherty
  David Emerson Hall
  David Lee Hollman
  James Edward Jones
  John Oscar Kerney
  Michael Lee Miller
  Emory Lee Rea
  Donald Ray Rhoades
  Larry Paul Stotler

William Henry Harrison High School
  Terry Wayne Booker
  Larry Hutton Bowers
  Jeffrey Lynn Buchanan
  Robert Clewlow
  Randall Allen Thompson
  Wayne Alan Wilcox

Mater Dei High School

  Thomas Leo McBride

Evansville Central High School
  William L. Armstrong
  Jack Allen Bowman
  Anthony William Dean
  Ronald Lee Groves
  Gerald Thomas Jenkins
  Bruce Edward Mileke
  Kerry Wayne Phillips

Evansville North High School
  John Gary Buchanan
  Ronald Lee Dempsey
  Ronald Lee Ellis
  Robert Mathew Fegan
  David Eugene Gill
  Richard H. Goheen
  Clarence Ray Husk
  Gary Blaine Jones
  William Junior Moore
  Charles Doyle Oglesby
  Danny Ray Schmidt

Memorial High School

Thomas Roger Keppen

Rex Mundi High School

David Frank Garrett
Mark Thomas Heavrin
Thomas Michael Koch
Ricahrd Allen Noelke
Raymond Anthony Wagner

Reitz High School

Robert Lee Baker
James Lisman Blackwell
Byron Dean Bonds
Chester Briscoe, Jr.
Gene Edmond Davis
Douglas Ray Harp
Randall Allen Henze
Michael Eugene Kraft
Thomas W. Reasor
Kenneth Eugene Slater

Note: I was unable to determine high schools attended of those not listed.

Evansville Vietnam Era Casualties by Military Unit

William Armstrong	3rd Marine Div., B Co., 1st Bat., 13th Marines
Robert Baker	4th Inf. Div., C Co., 3rd Bat., 8th Inf.
James Blackwell	25th Inf. Div., C Co., 2nd Bat., 35th Inf.
Sephen Boehne	198th Light Inf. Brig., A Co., 1st Bat., 6th Inf.
John Bohnsack	United States Army reserve, HHC, 168th Eng. Bat.
Byron Bonds	1st Marine Div., F Co., 2nd Bat., 1st Marines
Lewis Bonnie	1st Inf. Div., A Co., 2nd Bat., 1st Marines
Terry Booker	3rd Marine Div., L Co., 3rd Bat., 4th Marines
James Bowling	1st Marine Div., A Co., 1st Bat., 7th Marines
Chester Briscoe	3rd Marine Div., H & S Co., 2nd Bat., 4th Marines
Jeffrey Buchanan	3rd Marine Div., A Co., 1st Bat., 3rd Marines
John Buchanan	1st Cav. Div., Troop C, 1st Squad, 9th Cav.
Robert Clewlow	101st Airborne Div., A co., 1st Bat., 502nd Inf.
William Daughery	1st Mar. Div., F Co., 2nd Bat., 5th Marines
Gene Davis	4th Air Command Squadron
Anthony Dean	173rd Airborne Div., C Co., 4th Bat., 503rd Inf.
Ronald Dempsey	3rd Marine Div., B Co.,1st Bat., 13th Marines
Michael Dent	1st Cav. Div., C Co., 1st Bat., 12th Cav.
Ronald Ellis	3rd Marine Div., M Co., 3rd Bat., 3rd Marines
Robert Fegan	101st Airborne Div., HHC
David Garrett	3rd Marine Div., F Co., 2nd Bat., 4th Marines
David Gill	1st Aviation Brig., 118th Aviation Co., 145th Aviation Bat.

Richard Goheen	173rd Airborne Brig. 173rd Eng. Co.
Ronald Groves	1st Cav. Div., C Co., 2nd Bat., 7TH Cav.
David Hall	1st Marine Div., H & S Co., 1st Mountain Bat.
Donald Harp	3rd Marine Div., M Co., 3rd Bat., 3rd Marines
Thomas Heavrin	11th light Inf. Brig. C Co., 4th Bat., 3rd Inf.
Randall Henze	1st Cav. Div., D Co., 1st Bat., 7th Cav.
David Hollman	1st Marine Div., H & S Co., 3rd Bat., 1st Marines
Clarence Husk	25th Inf Div., Troop A, 3rd Squad, 4th Cav.
Gerald Jenkins	1st Inf. Div., B Co., 1st Bat., 28th Inf.
James Jones	1st Cav. Div., B Co., 229th Aviation Bat.
Gary Jones	101st Airborne Div., A Co., 2nd Bat., 502nd Inf.
Donald Kahre	11th light Inf Brig., B Co., 3rd Bat., 1st Inf.
Michael Kraft	1st Cav. Div., B Co., 1st Bat., 7th Cav.
Thomas Keppe	3rd Marine Div., B CO., 1st Bat., 1st Marines
John Kerney	1st Marine Div., B Co., 1st Bat., 1st Marines
Thomas Koch	1st Cav. Div., Troop C, 1st Squad, 9th Cav.
Thomas McBride	Unit Affiliation Not Reported
Charles McDaniels	Unit Affiliation Not Reported
Bruce Mielke	1st Marine Div., H & S Co., 3rd Bat., 5th Marines
George Moore	25th Inf., HHC, 4th Bat., 23rd Inf.
William Moore,	3rd Marine Div., E Co., 2nd Bat., 4th Marines
Charles Oglesby	1st Inf. Div., c Co., 2nd Bat., 16th Inf.
Kerry Phillips	20th Eng Brig., B Co., 31st Eng. Bat.
Emory Rea	9th Inf. Div., B Co., 5th Bat., 60th Inf.
Donald Rhodes	1st Inf. Div., A Co., 2nd Bat., 1st Inf.
Danny Schmidt	11th ACR, A Troop, 1st Squad, 11th Cav.

Kenneth Slater	25ht Inf., A co., 1st Bat., 27th Inf.
Larry Stotler	1st Cav. Div., D Troop, 1st Squadron, 9th Cav.
Randall Thompson	Americal Div., B Troop, 1st Squadron, 1st Cav.
Raymond Wagner	7th Air Force
Wayne Wilcox	9th Inf. Div., HHC, 2nd Bat., 47th Inf.
Donald Wilson	4th Inf. Div. HHB, 2nd Bat., 9th Artillery
Larry Bowers	1st Cav Div., C Co., 2nd Bat., 12th Cav.
Jack Bowman	1st Marine Div, D Co., 1st Bat., 26th Marines
Prentice Brenton	361st Reconnaissance Squadron
Lloyd Hyde	7th Fleet, CVW-16, TF 77
Leonard Lockard	571st Transportation Detachment
Thomas Metsker	1st Cav. Div., HHC, 1st Bat., 7th Cav.
Michael Miller	196th Light Inf. Brig., A Co., 2nd Bat., 1st Inf.
Dallas Moore	7th AirForce, 315th ACW, 311th ACS
Gerald Nicholson	III Maf, 1st MAW, Mag. 16, HMH 361
Richard Noelke	1st Cav. Div., HHC, 2nd Bat., 8th Cav.
Thomas Reasor	307th Strike Wing

Thomas Bitter and Ken Bowman are not listed due to not being Vietnam War casualties

Abbreviations

Bat.	Battalion
Brig.	Brigade
Cav.	Cavalry
Co.	Company

Div.   Division
Eng.   Engineering

MOS Codes-Vietnam Era

The U.S. military uses alphanumeric codes to identify the Military Occupational Specialty (MOS). The MOS that a person was qualified in was called the PMOS (primary MOS), while the DMOS (duty MOS) was the job they actually held at a given time. Most of the codes listed in this book are the DMOS held during their Vietnam tour.

Each branch of service had different types of codes. For the purpose of this book a detailed explanation of the meaning of each part of the code is not necessary. The codes below represent all the different MOS designations held by the Evansville casualties and how many Evansville soldiers had each MOS.

MOS Code	MOS defined	Number of soldiers
11B20	Infantryman (Specialist)	Twelve
0311	Rifleman	Eight
11B10	Infantryman (Basic)	Three
11B40	Infantryman (Non-com. officer)	Three
1542	Infantry Officer	Three
0341	Mortarman	Three
11B4P	Infantryman (P = Parachutist)	Two
3531	Motor Vehicle Operator	Two
11C10	Indirect Fire Infantryman	Two
0351	Assaultman	Two

1371	Combat Engineer	One
100B	Utility/Observation Helicopter Pilot	One
43191	Aircraft Maintenance Superintendent	One
2P40	Brass Group Leader (Musician), PMOS	One
62B20	Construction Equipment Repairer	One
11E20	Armor Crewman	One
67A1F	Aircraft Maintenance	One
11B1P	Infantryman (P=Parachutist)	One
0302	Infantry Officer	One
0331	Machinegunner	One
31G40	Tactical Communications Chief	One
11C20	Indirect Fire Infantryman	One
12B40	Combat Engineer	One
11B2V	Infantryman (Unsure about 2V designation)	One
11H10	Infantry Direct Fire Crewman	One
1204	Armored Reconnaissance Unit Commander	One
71193	Field Artillery Unit Commander	One
2105	Air Warfare Research Officer	One
62D220	Asphalt Equipment Operator	One
6321	Aircraft Communications	One

Note: Some of the soldiers did not have their MOS reported.

About the Proceeds Beneficiaries

All Proceed from this work will go to three beneficiaries. They are the Vietnam Veteran's Memorial Fund (VVMF), VFW Post 1114 in Evansville, IN, and the Jennifer Solomon Hope Fund.

Although I have been interested in the Vietnam War since I was in elementary school the VVMF is where I was able to put my interest into action in my role as a history teacher. I became an inaugural member of the Teach Vietnam Teachers' Network in 2002. As I observed the work with which the fund is involved in keeping the legacy of the Wall and the war alive, I was very impressed with the organization. When I traveled to Vietnam in 2005 and saw the work of Project Renew, which is helping rid Quang Tri Province of deadly unexploded ordnance (UXO) I felt the need to find a way to help this effort. Through sale of this book I hope to do just a small part.

The VFW Post 1114 has the largest membership of any VFW Post in the world. Members of the post provide color guards for many military related functions including the rededication ceremony that my students planned and organized in 2003. Post 1114 has provided innumerable services to veterans over many years. I believe they are a great choice to receive a portion of the proceeds because they have contact with so many veterans.

The Jennifer Solomon Hope Fund was set up for Jennifer and her girls after Jennifer became gravely ill. In the time of one month she went from perfect health to having one leg amputated just below the knee and one just above the knee. Her right thumb was partially amputated and she had serious damage to tendon and muscle tissue in her hands, which severely limited their use. In a little over two years since this tragedy Jennifer has learned to walk with prosthetics, learned to drive, and has returned to work part-time as a special education teacher. She has had numerous surgeries and continues with therapy to improve the use of her hands. Jennifer lives in Madison, WI with her two girls Madison age 16 and Rea age 13. Jennifer is definitely a worthwhile beneficiary of portions of these proceeds. She is in a situation very similar to many of our returning injured veterans and has attended amputee conferences where she has met some of these veterans. Jennifer hopes to further her education and become a clinical counselor for disabled citizens. She would also like to speak to school groups. Jennifer became ill with a rare disorder called PurPura fulminas and is only the fourth known survivor. Jennifer Solomon is my sister-in-law.

About the Vietnam Veterans Memorial-Washington D.C.

"The Wall" was completed and dedicated in 1982. It was the idea of Jan Scruggs, a decorated Vietnam veteran. All of the funding for the memorial came by way of private donations and most in small amounts by thousands of ordinary citizens. The Vietnam Veterans Memorial Fund is a non-profit organization whose purpose is to keep alive the legacy of the memorial wall and to promote education and healing. It is funded by private donations.

The final design for the memorial was chosen from around 10,000 entries. The winning design came from a twenty-year-old architectural design student name Maya Lin. It was controversial at first to some as being too somber. A compromise was reached concerning this issue when a more traditional element, a statue depicting three combat soldiers, was added as part of the memorial.

Maya Lin's idea of listing the names chronologically by date of casualty is one of the most important design elements. In the event of many soldiers getting killed in one battle, surviving soldiers can come to the wall and find their comrades in arms close together on the wall. As of 2007 there were 58,256 names on the wall.

The story of Jan Scruggs and his quest to have this memorial built is told in a movie entitled "To Heal A Nation". To learn more about the Vietnam Veterans Memorial go to www.vvmf.org.

About the Vietnam Veterans Memorial-Washington D.C. 81

Author at military museum, DaNang, Vietnam

Conclusion

"There is nothing glorious about war. It causes nothing but pain, death, and destruction," said Art Borgquist a Vietnam veteran and teacher in California. Every year he does a Memorial Day lesson focused specifically on the Vietnam era and the theme that freedom is not free. Whether one agrees or not as to how much of a threat Vietnam posed to our freedom, or currently Iraq, we must understand the high cost of war in human terms and how it affects us all.

I hope this book helps keep alive the much too short histories of these men, and readers get a sense of how much was lost with each of these lives. The number of casualties from Evansville, 67, is an interesting number because it represents just slightly more than one tenth of one percent of the total number of Vietnam casualties. So multiply Evansville's loss and pain by one thousand to understand what the nation lost.

To all veterans who read this book and especially Vietnam veterans, "WELCOME HOME."

Sources

A Walk in the Clouds. Film by David Kniess Jr. http://zoiibeanpictures.com

Evansville Courier. obituaries compiled by Charles Browning. Maintained by the Evansville Public Library. electronic data base. Browning genealogy database. http//browning.evpl.org

Evansville Press. Obituaries compiled by Charles Browning. Maintained by the Evansville Public Library. Electronic database. Browning genealogy database. http//browning.evpl.org

GIsearch.com. www.gisearch.com/memorial/vietnam.

The National Archives. www.aad.archives.gov./aad/

Vietnam Veterans Memorial Fund. Echoes From The Wall Poster. www.vvmf.org.

978-0-595-50222-6
0-595-50222-9